ISAAC ASIMOV'S
Library of the Universe

JUPITER:
The Spotted Giant

by Isaac Asimov

Gareth Stevens Publishing
Milwaukee

Library of Congress Cataloging-in-Publication Data

Asimov, Isaac, 1920-
    Jupiter, the spotted giant.

    (Isaac Asimov's Library of the universe)
    Bibliography: p.
    Includes index.
    Summary: Introduces the largest planet, one composed largely of gases and having numerous satellites.
    1. Jupiter (Planet) --Juvenile literature.
[1. Jupiter (Planet)] I. Title. II. Series: Asimov, Isaac, 1920-
Library of the universe.
QB661.A843   1989   523.4'5   88-42893
ISBN 1-55532-363-4

A Gareth Stevens Children's Books edition

Edited, designed, and produced by
Gareth Stevens, Inc. 7317 West Green Tree Road Milwaukee, Wisconsin 53223, USA

Text copyright © 1989 by Nightfall, Inc.
End matter copyright © 1989 by Gareth Stevens, Inc.
Format copyright © 1989 by Gareth Stevens, Inc.

Cover art © Julian Baum
Project editor: Mark Sachner
Designer: Laurie Shock
Research editor: Scott Enk
Picture research: Matthew Groshek
Technical advisers and consulting editors: Julian Baum and Francis Reddy

1 2 3 4 5 6 7 8 9 94 93 92 91 90 89

Printed in the United States of America

CONTENTS

Nowadays, we have seen planets up close, all the way to distant Uranus. We have mapped Venus through its clouds. We have seen craters on Mercury and dead volcanoes on Mars. We have detected strange objects no one knew anything about until recently: quasars, pulsars, black holes. We have learned amazing facts about how stars explode and about how the Universe was born, and we have some ideas about how it may die. Nothing can be more astonishing and more interesting.

Within our own Solar system, the family of planets that circle the Sun, we have the largest planet, Jupiter, rightly named for the king of gods in ancient Roman myths. It is an enormous world that dwarfs our own Earth, and everything about it is extreme — its atmosphere, its storms, its temperature, its satellites. In this book, we will learn about this giant planet.

Isaac Asimov

The "Discovery" of Jupiter

Jupiter is normally the fourth brightest object in the sky. Only the Sun, Earth's Moon, and Venus are brighter. Jupiter has been seen from the earliest times. In 1610, an Italian scientist, Galileo (pronounced gal-ill-AY-o), looked at Jupiter with a small telescope. Near it he saw four dimmer objects. Night after night they moved back and forth from one side of Jupiter to the other.

These objects were satellites, or moons — smaller bodies that circled Jupiter the way our Moon circles Earth. These were the first moons discovered that were seen to circle some body other than Earth.

Above: one of Galileo's original sketches of Jupiter and its moons.

Right: Galileo Galilei, Italian astronomer and scientist.

4

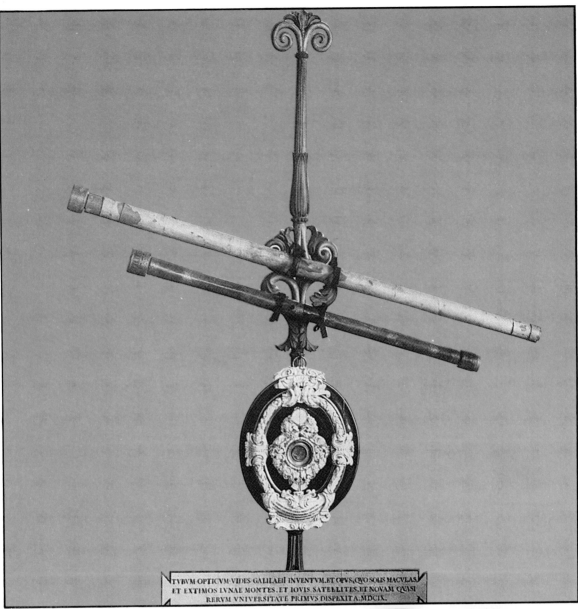

Galileo's homemade telescopes (above) could barely show him Jupiter's moons. Today, a good pair of binoculars (right) can reveal them.

See for Yourself

Jupiter orbits the Sun about once every 12 years. It stays in the zodiac, which is the circle of 12 constellations along which the Sun and Moon move, too. Astronomy magazines can tell you where Jupiter will be from night to night in the current month.

If you look at Jupiter through a small telescope, you will see that instead of looking like a bright dot, it will look like a little disk of light. Nearby, you might see Jupiter's four largest satellites, some on one side, some on the other. From night to night you will see the positions of the satellites change as they move about Jupiter.

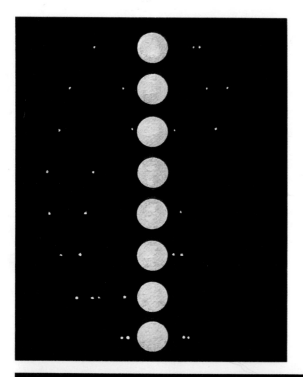

Left: Jupiter as viewed through binoculars. Jupiter's four largest moons play hide-and-seek as they circle their parent planet over the course of eight nights, June 1 (top) through June 8 (bottom), 1988.

Below: Jupiter and the same four family members as viewed through a small telescope.

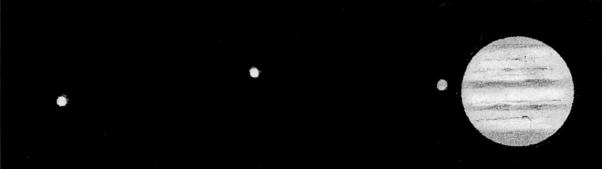

If Galileo could spot Jupiter, so can you. All it takes is a clear night and a pair of binoculars or a small telescope for a fascinating look at the giant of our Solar system.

A rocky core — about the size of our own planet — may lie at Jupiter's center. Above this is a vast layer of liquid hydrogen, which makes up most of Jupiter's mass. The upper atmosphere contains ammonia, methane, and water vapor. (See enlarged "slice.")

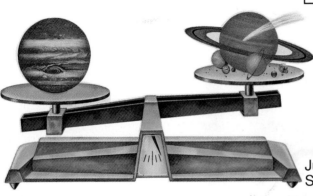

Jupiter outweighs all the other planets in the Solar system.

This Is Jupiter

With a diameter of 88,700 miles (142,718 km), Jupiter is the largest planet in our Solar system. It is more than 11 times wider than Earth, and it contains 318 times as much mass as Earth — and more than two-thirds of the total mass of the nine known planets. Even though Jupiter is so large, it spins much faster than Earth does. It makes one full turn on its axis in just under 10 hours.

Scientists have sent space probes (Pioneers 10 and 11, and Voyagers 1 and 2) past Jupiter. These probes have taken close-up photographs of Jupiter's surface and have shown that the planet is a huge ball composed mainly of the two simplest gases — mostly hydrogen plus some helium. The upper atmosphere also contains vapors of substances like water, methane, and ammonia.

Fierce Winds and Swirling Storms

Through a large telescope, Jupiter's surface is seen to be covered with dark "belts" and lighter "zones" between them. These are the result of atmospheric movements. Vast winds move upward in the zones and downward in the belts.

Along the belts and zones are light and dark oval spots that represent enormous whirling storm winds. The largest of these is called the Great Red Spot. This huge feature of Jupiter seems to be a gigantic hurricane that never stops. Astronomers have watched it whirling now for over 300 years!

Jupiter's Great Red Spot (left) and a storm on Earth (right). Although their scales are vastly different, the same laws of nature give them similar appearances.

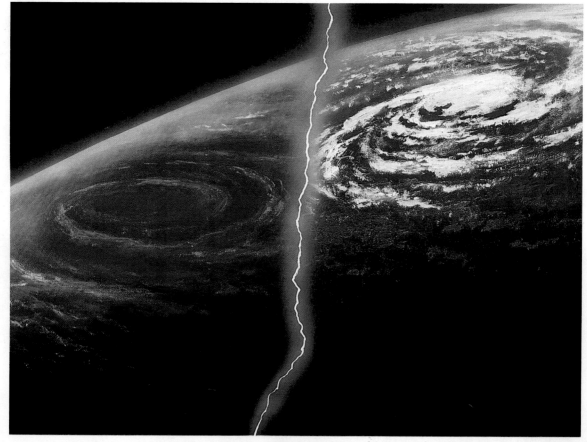

The Great Red Spot could swallow several Earths!

**The Great Red Spot —
nothing on Earth can compare**

Even Jupiter's <u>parts</u> are huge! The Great Red Spot, which seems to be a huge storm, is about 25,000 miles (40,000 km) from east to west and 8,000 miles (13,000 km) north to south. So if you took three Earth-size planets, you could drop all three side by side into that huge storm at once without touching the edges. The area of the Great Red Spot —175,000,000 square miles (453,250,000 sq km) — is over three times the size of all Earth's continents put together!

Jupiter's Ring

Giant planets far from the Sun have material nearby that condenses, or collects, into satellites. If the material is too close to the planet, however, the planet's gravity keeps the material from condensing. The material then forms a ring of small pieces around the planet.

The planet Saturn has very large, bright rings of this sort. Astronomers have known about Saturn's rings since the 1600s, when Galileo first saw through his telescope what looked like "ears" around Jupiter's neighbor.

But Jupiter had a surprise for astronomers — a surprise that went undetected until 1979. That's when Voyager 1 discovered a thin ring of debris about 30,000 miles (48,000 km) above Jupiter's cloudy edge. Jupiter's ring is too dim to be seen from Earth. Jupiter has at least one "shepherd satellite"— a small moon whose gravity keeps the ring from spreading outward and disappearing.

Left: The view from Jupiter's ring. Sunlight scattered by the ring's tiny particles creates the appearance of a rainbow in space.

Below: Voyager 2's cameras photographed part of Jupiter's dust ring in 1979.

Above: Jupiter's dust ring is too faint to be seen from Earth. An artist added it to this picture of Jupiter to show the ring's size and location.

The Great Red Spot — a storm with a mind of its own?

Many mysteries surround the Great Red Spot. For one thing, scientists are not certain why it has lasted for centuries. Other storms come and go, but the Great Red Spot seems to be permanent. Scientists also wonder about the Great Red Spot's movement. It can move ahead or fall behind the rest of the clouds. It moves only east and west and not north and south. Recent experiments with swirling liquids might answer some questions, but we still aren't sure.

Jupiter's Family

Jupiter has 16 known satellites. Of these, the four largest are called the Galilean (gal-ill-AY-en) satellites, in honor of Galileo, who is usually credited with discovering them. But they were named by a German astronomer, Simon Marius, who actually spotted them a few days before Galileo did. The nearest of these to Jupiter is Io. Beyond Io are Europa, Ganymede, and Callisto. Each of the Galilean satellites is about the size of our Moon, or larger.

Far outside the orbits of these four satellites are at least eight smaller moons, from 12 to 105 miles (19 to 169 km) across. They are probably captured asteroids. Closer to Jupiter than the four large satellites is a small satellite called Amalthea, which is about 125 miles (201 km) across. Near it are three even smaller satellites that were discovered by the probes.

Let's take a closer look at the Galilean moons for a view of both the variety and similarities among Jupiter's family of little worlds.

Opposite: Shown not according to size but in their correct positions, Jupiter and the Galilean satellites "pose" for a family portrait, taken by Voyager 1. Clockwise from upper left: Callisto, Ganymede, Io, and Jupiter. Center: Europa.

Inset, opposite: Who's who in the Jupiter system? This painting and the map below show the orbits of Jupiter's moons, big and small.

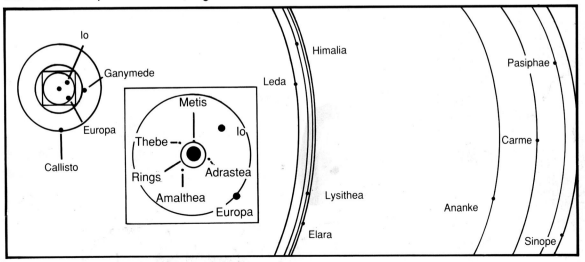

Callisto — A Distant Moon

Callisto, the farthest of the Galilean satellites from Jupiter, is 1,168,000 miles (1,879,312 km) from the planet. That's almost five times as far as our Moon is from us! Callisto travels around Jupiter in about 16 2/3 days.

The probes have shown that Callisto is a big ball of ice with some rock, though it may have a rocky core. Callisto is thickly covered with craters, showing that billions of years ago, when it was first created, Callisto was bombarded by the final chunks of matter that formed it.

The craters are not very deep, because the icy surface slowly flowed and settled. But the flow wasn't enough to wipe out the craters altogether. So thanks to Callisto's icy craters, we have been able to peek back to the early days of our Solar system.

Callisto's craters were revealed by the Voyager probes.

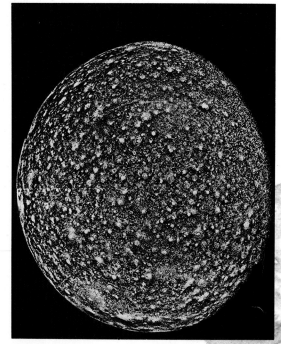

Below: a familiar sight — partially melted Earth ice. Callisto is a big ball of ice. The impacts of the objects that made the craters created so much heat that the frozen surface partially melted, then refroze.

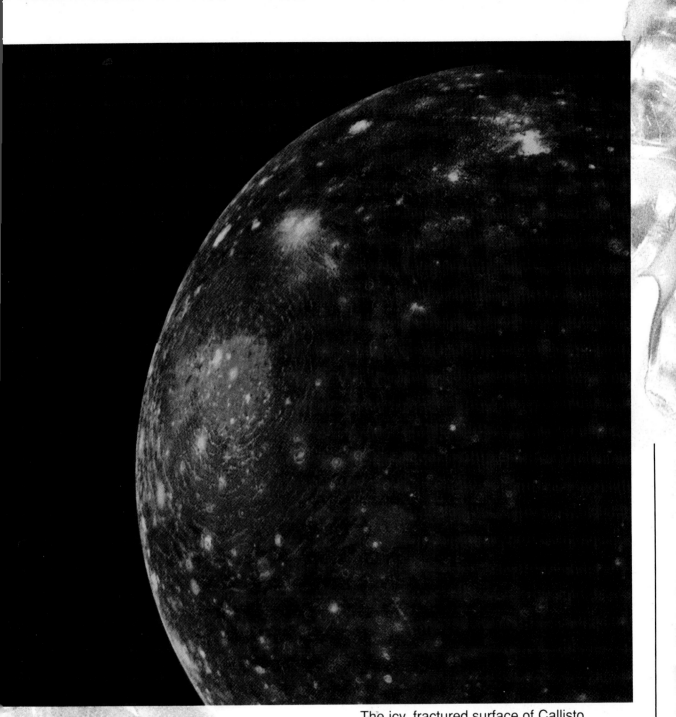

The icy, fractured surface of Callisto, photographed by Voyager 1 in 1979. Notice the bright ringed region near the moon's left edge — the remains of a violent impact that partially melted Callisto's frozen surface. The bright region is nearly 185 miles (300 km) across.

The view from Ganymede, the largest satellite in the Solar system.

Ganymede — A Moon Bigger Than Mercury

Ganymede, the largest satellite in the Solar system, is nearly 3,300 miles (5,310 km) across. It is considerably larger than our Moon, and it is even larger than the planet Mercury. But like Callisto, Ganymede is mostly ice with some rock, whereas Mercury is rock and metal. For that reason Mercury is heavier, or more massive, than Ganymede.

Ganymede is 665,000 miles (about 1,070,000 km) from Jupiter. It takes just over a week for Ganymede to orbit its planet. Ganymede is not covered as thickly with craters as Callisto is. That may be because Ganymede's crust seems to have cracked and shifted in many places over a long period of time. Water from inside Ganymede may have welled up, flooded many craters, and then frozen smoothly over its surface.

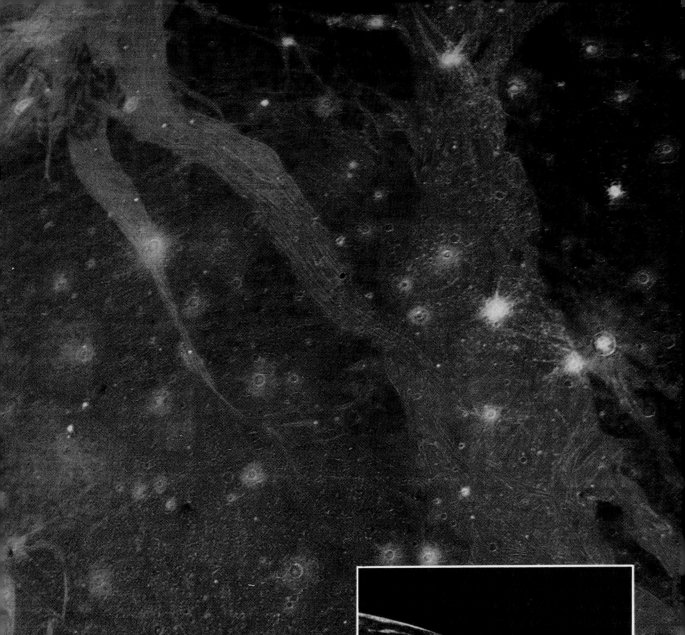

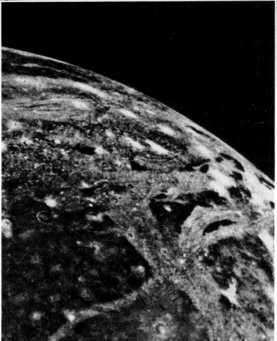

Above: Craters old and new pepper
Ganymede. Bright patches showing "rays"
of debris (right center) are fresh craters.
Fainter circular markings (center) may be
ancient craters smoothed over by glacier-
like flows on Ganymede's icy surface.

Right: Strange "grooved" terrain runs
across Ganymede. The grooves are
probably cracks caused by slow expansion
and movement of Ganymede's crust.

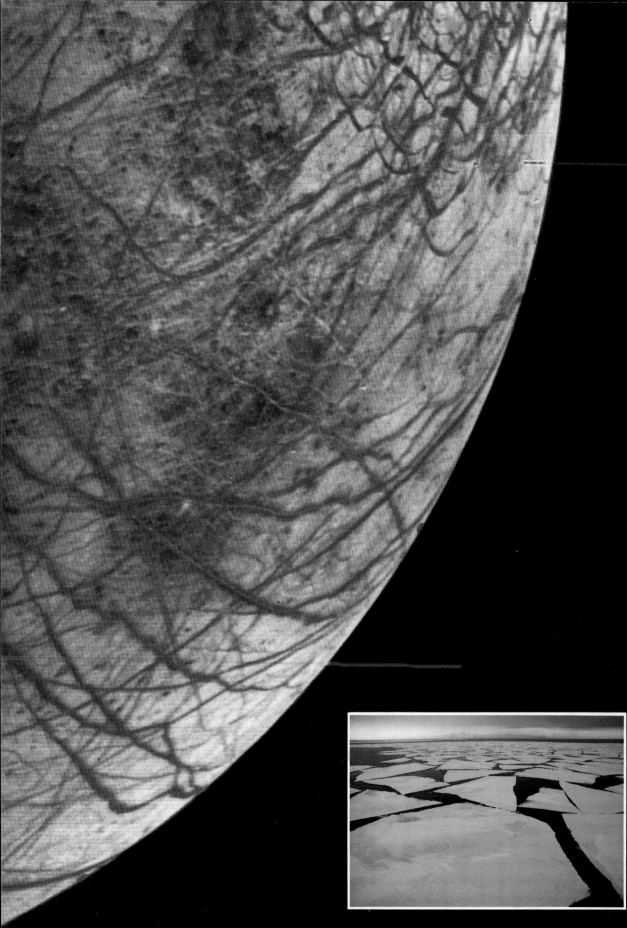

Europa — A Glacial Moon

Europa is the smallest of the four Galilean satellites — only 1,942 miles (3,125 km) across, or a little smaller than our Moon. It is about 417,000 miles (671,000 km) from Jupiter and orbits the planet in a little over 3.5 days. The probes show that it doesn't have many craters, but seems to be covered with a smooth sheet of ice, a global glacier. There may even be liquid water underneath.

If a meteorite strikes Europa, it cracks the ice so that water moves up and freezes, wiping out any crater that might have formed. Pictures sent back by the Voyager probes show that the glacier is cracked all over.

Opposite: Europa's smooth icy surface is scarred by the impact of countless meteorites. This image was photographed by Voyager 2. Inset: huge masses of ice — pack ice — float off the coast of Antarctica.

Below: an artist's concept of an ice-water volcano on Europa. Could a gigantic liquid ocean lie beneath Europa's icy surface?

Top inset: Parícutin, a Mexican volcano, began as a smoking mound in a cornfield.

Bottom inset: Artist's concept of a volcanic eruption on Io.

Io — A Volcanic Moon

Io, which orbits Jupiter in a little over 1 3/4 days, is only a little bigger than our Moon. It is about 262,000 miles (421,560 km) from Jupiter, which makes it only a little farther from Jupiter than our Moon is from us. In fact, Io is so near Jupiter that Jupiter's gravitational pull stretches and heats it. For that reason, any ice it may have had has disappeared, and Io is now simply a ball of rocky material. It is even hot enough to have volcanoes!

We have pictures from our probes that show these volcanoes in action, spewing out sulfur. The sulfur covers the surface, turns it yellow, and wipes out any craters that may have formed.

Opposite: A sulfurous plume of material rises high above one of Io's many volcanoes.
Below: The tortured, sulfurous surface of Io.

23

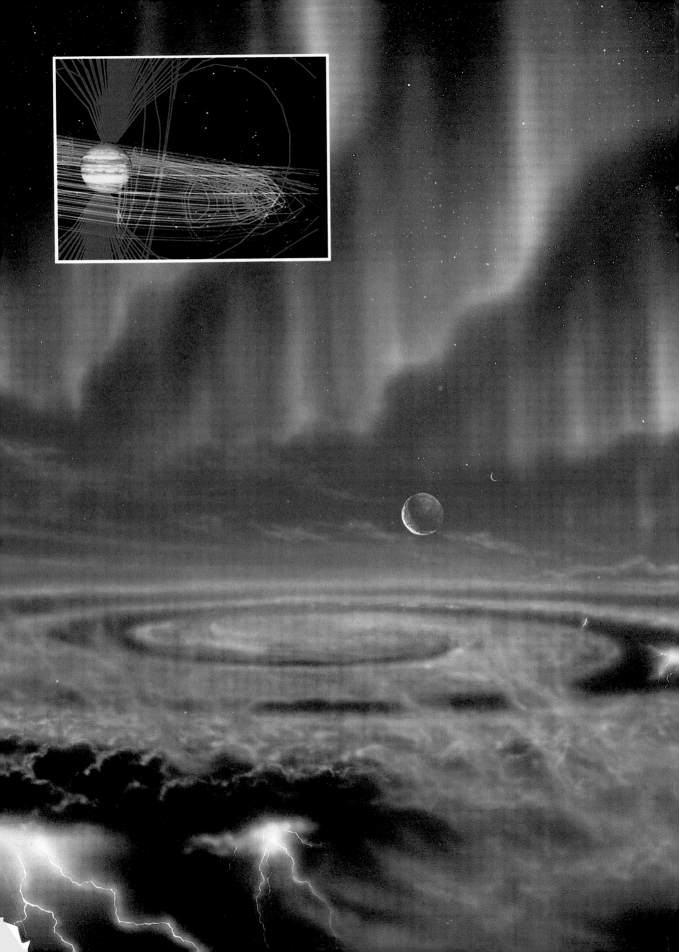

What Have We Learned?

The probes have told us much about Jupiter that we couldn't have learned otherwise. For instance, we now know that Jupiter is surrounded by a magnetic field much larger and stronger than Earth's. The field is so strong and collects so many charged particles that spaceships with human beings aboard might have to stay far away from Jupiter.

The probes also showed us that although the surface of Jupiter's cloud layer is very cold, the temperature rises rapidly as one penetrates below it. Thousands of miles below its cloud layer, Jupiter is hotter than the surface of the Sun!

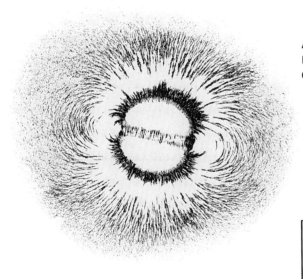

A do-it-yourself magnetic field: a powerful magnet placed under a sheet of paper covered with iron filings.

Opposite: an artist's concept of a spectacular display in Jupiter's nighttime sky. The fierce lightning and streamers of light similar to the aurora on Earth surpass in size and brilliance anything likely to be seen in our planet's atmosphere.

Inset, opposite: a computer image of Jupiter's intense magnetic field (shown in blue). Also shown (in yellow) is a donut-shaped trail of sulfur left by Io, Jupiter's volcanic moon.

Jupiter — brought to you in living color. But why?

Jupiter is a very colorful planet. The belts are orange, yellow, and brown. There are white spots, and, of course, there is the Great Red Spot, which isn't always red. Sometimes, its color pales until it can hardly be seen. The thing is, though, that scientists are not certain as to exactly what causes the colors. What gases are present? What chemical changes take place? We will have answers when we drop instruments into the atmosphere.

25

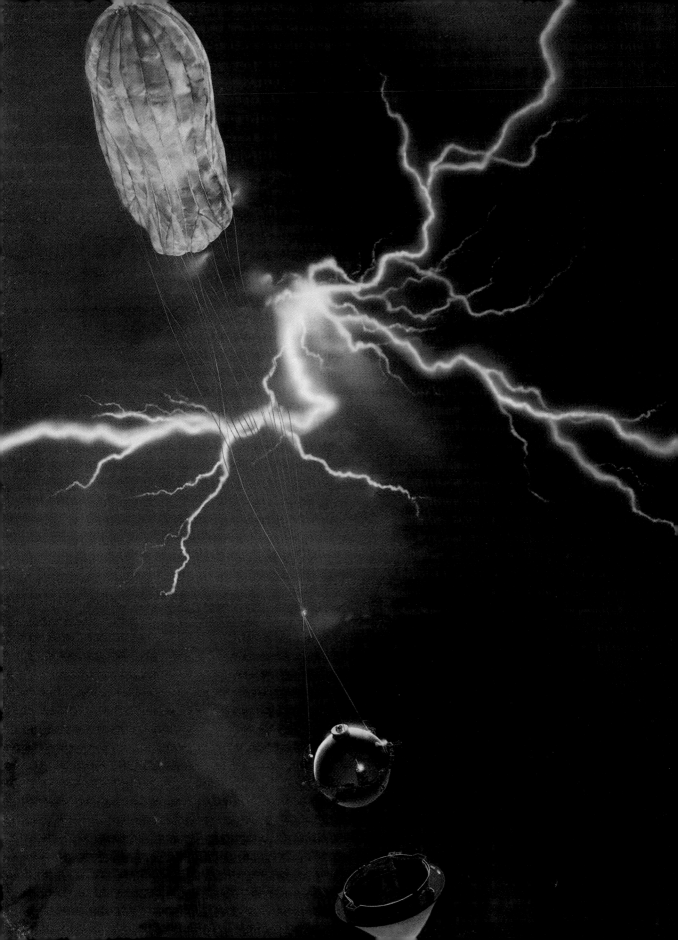

Closing in on Jupiter

Some day, scientists hope to put a probe in orbit around Jupiter. From such a probe, a package of instruments can be dropped into Jupiter's atmosphere. It might then be possible to get accurate information about the substances that make up Jupiter and their temperatures.

Perhaps we can land instruments on one of the small outer satellites that are outside Jupiter's powerful magnetic field and set up a long-term study of the planet. Other probes might be sent skimming by Jupiter's atmosphere to collect helium, a valuable gas that Earth may run out of some day.

Thanks to the Pioneer and Voyager probes, we've learned much about Jupiter in a very short time. And with the Galileo probe set to further explore the planet, who knows what new mysteries will soon be revealed about Jupiter, the giant among the gas giants?

Opposite: Separating from its heat shield, the Galileo atmospheric probe begins its long fall through Jupiter's atmosphere.

Jupiter's center —
a kind of inner Sun?

Some scientists think Jupiter may be hydrogen and helium all through. But many others do not think these gases are present all the way to the center. They think there is a ball of rock and metal at the very center that could be only as large as Earth, but right now there's no way of telling. Then, too, the center may be squeezed so hard that heat is produced there. We do know that Jupiter actually produces more heat than it receives from the Sun!

Fact File: Jupiter

Our Solar system's largest known planet is the fifth closest to the Sun. Like the Sun, Jupiter is mostly hydrogen and helium. Scientists believe that the temperature at its core might be as much as 55,000°F (about 30,500°C). When it was formed over 4.5 billion years ago, Jupiter might have given off 10 million times as much energy as it does now. Jupiter was never massive enough to begin the process stars use to burn their hydrogen. But billions of years ago, it might have glowed like a miniature star!

The Moons of Jupiter

Name	Metis	Adrastea	Amalthea	Thebe	Io
Diameter	25 miles* (40 km)*	15 miles (24 km)	162 miles** (260 km)**	62 miles (100 km)	2,256 miles (3,632 km)
Distance From Jupiter's Center	79,500 miles (128,000 km)	80,000 miles (128,700 km)	112,700 miles (181,300 km)	137,900 miles (221,900 km)	262,000 miles (421,600 km)

Name	Europa	Ganymede	Callisto	Leda	Himalia
Diameter	1,942 miles (3,126 km)	3,278 miles (5,276 km)	2,995 miles (4,820 km)	12 miles (20 km)	105 miles (170 km)
Distance From Jupiter's Center	416,900 miles (670,900 km)	665,000 miles (1,070,000 km)	1,168,000 miles (1,880,000 km)	6,904,000 miles (11,110,000 km)	7,127,000 miles (11,470,000 km)

* Estimated diameter
** Diameter at widest point

Jupiter: How It Measures Up to Earth

Planet	Diameter	Rotation Period
Jupiter	88,700 miles (142,718 km)	9 hours, 50.4 minutes
Earth	7,926 miles (12,756 km)	23 hours, 56 minutes

The Sun and Its Family of Planets

The Sun and its Solar system family, left to right: Mercury, Venus, Earth, Mars, Jupiter, Saturn, Uranus, Neptune, Pluto. Left: Here is a close-up of Jupiter and its seven largest moons (left to right), Himalia, Callisto, Ganymede, Europa, Io, Thebe, Amalthea.

Lysithea	Elara	Ananke	Carme	Pasiphae	Sinope
19 miles (30 km)	47 miles (76 km)	19 miles (30 km)	25 miles (40 km)	31 miles (50 km)	25 miles (40 km)
7,277,000 miles (11,710,000 km)	7,295,000 miles (11,740,000 km)	12,850,000 miles (20,700,000 km)	13,900,000 miles (22,350,000 km)	14,500,000 miles (23,300,000 km)	14,750,000 miles (23,700,000 km)

Period of Orbit Around Sun (length of year)	Moons	Surface Gravity	Distance from Sun (nearest-farthest)	Least Time It Takes for Light to Travel to Earth
11.86 years	at least 16	2.53*	460.5-507.0 million miles (740.9-815.7 million km)	32.75 minutes
365.25 days (one year)	1	1.00*	92-95 million miles (147-152 million km)	—

* Multiply your weight by this number to find out how much you would weigh on this planet.

More Books About Jupiter

Here are more books that contain information about Jupiter. If you are interested in them, check your library or bookstore.

The Giant Planets. Nourse (Franklin Watts)
Jupiter. Simon (Morrow Junior Books)
Our Solar System. Asimov (Gareth Stevens)
Our Wonderful Solar System. Adams (Troll)
The Planets. Couper (Franklin Watts)
Planets. Radlauer and Stembridge (Childrens Press)
Planets and the Solar System. Brandt (Troll)
Rockets, Probes, and Satellites. Asimov (Gareth Stevens)

Places to Visit

You can explore Jupiter and other parts of the Universe without leaving Earth. Here are some museums and centers where you can find a variety of space exhibits.

Astrocentre — Royal Ontario Museum
Toronto, Ontario

Andrus Planetarium — Hudson River Museum
Yonkers, New York

NASA Goddard Space Flight Center
Greenbelt, Maryland

Dow Planetarium
Montreal, Quebec

Kansas Cosmosphere and Space Center
Hutchinson, Kansas

NASA Ames Research Center
Moffett Field, California

McDonald Observatory
Austin and Fort Davis, Texas

NASA John F. Kennedy Space Center
Kennedy Space Center, Florida

For More Information About Jupiter

Here are some people you can write to for more information about Jupiter. Be sure to tell them exactly what you want to know about or see. Remember to include your age, full name, and address.

For information about Jupiter:
National Space Society
600 Maryland Avenue, SW
Washington, DC 20024

The Planetary Society
65 North Catalina
Pasadena, California 91106

About missions to Jupiter:
NASA Jet Propulsion Laboratory
Public Affairs 180-201
4800 Oak Grove Drive
Pasadena, California 91109

The Space and Rocket Center
Space Camp Applications
One Tranquility Base
Huntsville, Alabama 35807

For catalogs of posters, slides, and other astronomy materials:
AstroMedia Order Department
1027 N. 7th Street
Milwaukee, Wisconsin 53233

Selectory Sales
Astronomical Society of the Pacific
1290 24th Avenue
San Francisco, California 94122

Glossary

asteroid: "star-like." Asteroids are very small planets made of rock or metal. There are thousands of them in our Solar system. They mainly orbit the Sun in large numbers between Mars and Jupiter, but some are found in other parts of the Solar system.

atmosphere: the gases that surround a planet, star, or moon.

axis: the imaginary straight line about which a planet, star, or moon turns or spins.

billion: in North America — and in this book — the number represented by 1 followed by nine zeroes — 1,000,000,000. In some places, such as the United Kingdom (Britain), this number is called "a thousand million." In these places, one billion would then be represented by 1 followed by *12* zeroes — 1,000,000,000,000: a million million, a number known as a trillion in North America.

black hole: a massive object — usually a collapsed star — so tightly packed that not even light can escape the force of its gravity.

captured asteroids: asteroids that have been trapped by the gravity of other planets. They then circle the larger planet.

comet: an object made of ice, rock, and gas. It has a vapor trail that may be seen when the comet's orbit brings it close to the Sun.

constellation: a grouping of stars in the sky that seems to trace a familiar pattern or figure. Constellations are often named after the shapes they resemble.

crater: a hole or pit in the surface of a planet or moon caused by volcanic explosion or the impact of a meteorite.

Galilean satellites: Jupiter's four largest satellites — Io, Europa, Ganymede, and Callisto — which Galileo studied through his telescope. Each of them is about the size of Earth's Moon, or larger.

Galileo: an Italian astronomer who developed the use of the telescope to study the four largest moons of Jupiter, sunspots, mountains on the Moon, the phases of Venus, and many other objects and events in the Universe.

glacier: an enormous layer of ice formed from compacted snow, often itself carrying a layer of snow.

Great Red Spot: the largest of the huge whirling storms that move along the "belts" and "zones" of Jupiter's surface.

helium: a light, colorless gas that makes up part of every star.

hydrogen: a colorless, odorless gas that is the simplest and lightest of the elements. Most stars are three-quarters hydrogen.

rings: the bands of ice, rock, and dust particles that circle some planets, including Jupiter, at their equators.

satellite: a smaller body orbiting a larger body. Ganymede is Jupiter's largest <u>natural</u> satellite. Sputnik 1 was Earth's first <u>artificial</u> satellite.

"shepherd satellites": small moons, or moonlets, that orbit within or near Jupiter's rings. Their weak gravity helps keep ring matter from drifting out of position.

sulfur: a pale yellow element that can be used to make gunpowder and certain kinds of medication.

vapor: a gas formed from a solid or liquid. On Earth, clouds are made of water vapor.

zodiac: the band of 12 constellations across the sky that represents the paths of the Sun, the Moon, Mercury, Venus, Mars, Jupiter, and Saturn.

Index

The publishers wish to thank the following for permission to reproduce copyright material: front cover, © Julian Baum, 1988; pp. 4, 5 (upper), AIP Niels Bohr Library; p. 5 (lower), photograph courtesy of Celestron International; pp. 6, 6-7 (lower), © Richard Baum, 1988; p. 7, © Garret Moore, 1988; pp. 8, 9, © Lynette Cook, 1988; pp. 10, 24 (full page), © John Foster, 1988; pp. 11, 14 (full page), 19 (upper), 20 (full page), photographs courtesy of NASA; pp. 12 (left), 21, © Michael Carroll; pp. 12-13 (lower), 16 (left), 17 (upper), 19 (inset), 22 (large), 23, Jet Propulsion Laboratory; pp. 13 (upper), 24 (inset), 26, courtesy of NASA; p. 14 (inset), © George Peirson, 1988; p. 15, Sabine Huschke/© Gareth Stevens, Inc.; pp. 16-17 (lower), 25, Matthew Groshek/© Gareth Stevens, Inc.; p. 18, © Ron Miller; p. 20 (inset), © M. P. Kahl/Tom Stack and Associates; p. 22 (upper inset), United States Geological Survey; p. 22 (lower inset), © MariLynn Flynn, 1987; pp. 28-29, © Sally Bensusen, 1987; p. 29 (inset), © Sally Bensusen, 1988.